IN
CATASTROPHE
CALLING!

ANDI WATSON

WALKER

To my own personal superheroes,
Philippa and Clara

This is a work of fiction. Names, characters, places and incidents
are either the product of the author's imagination or, if real, used fictitiously.

First published 2012 by Walker Books Ltd

87 Vauxhall Walk, London SE11 5HJ

2 4 6 8 10 9 7 5 3 1

Text & Illustrations © 2012 Andi Watson

The right of Andi Watson to be identified as author of this work has been asserted by him
in accordance with the Copyright, Designs and Patents Act 1988

This book has been typeset in Block T

Printed and bound in China

British Library Cataloguing in Publication Data: a catalogue record for this
book is available from the British Library

ISBN 978-1-4063-2939-1

www.walker.co.uk   www.gumgirl.co.uk

8

9

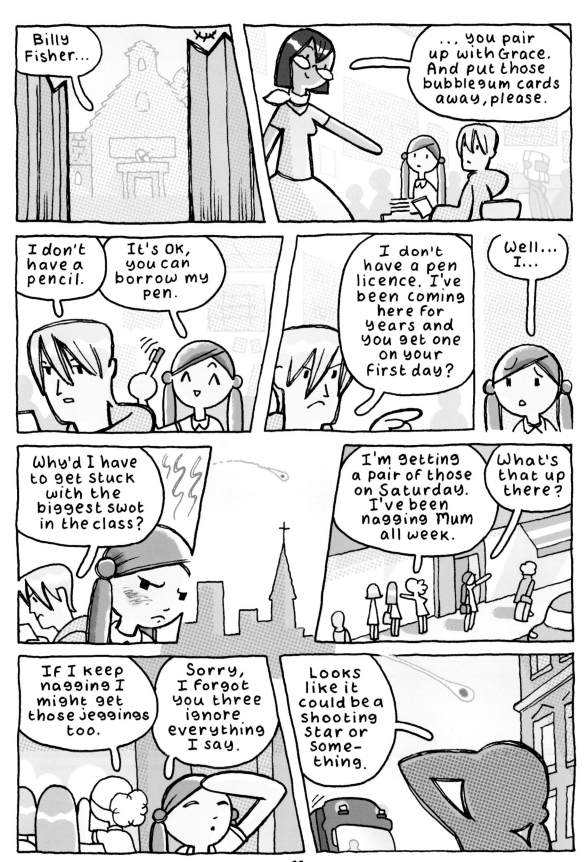

Oh my...

That.
Was.
Close.

Grace, you're the luckiest...

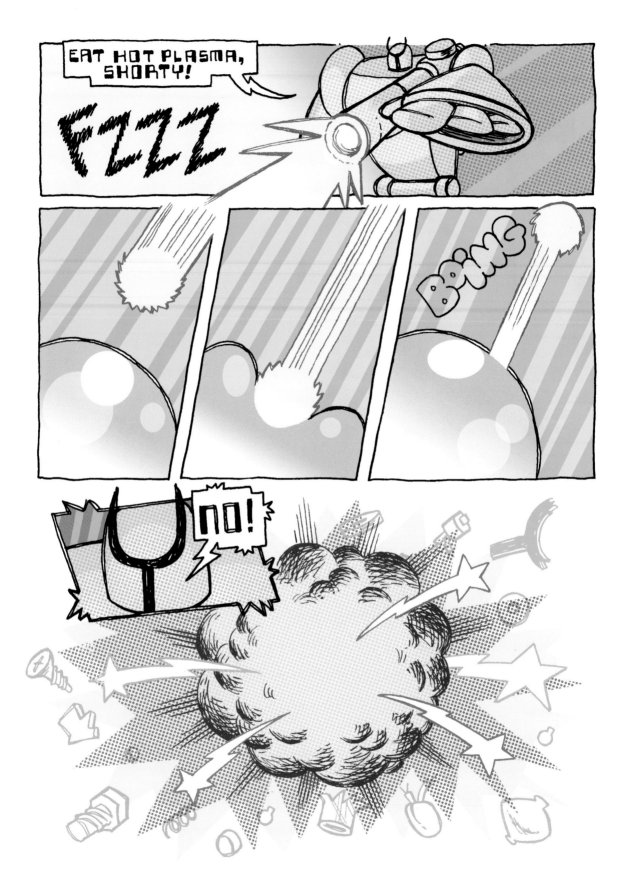

CALAMITY PRIMARY SCHOOL

Are we in time, Billy?

Just.

They should be about to start their meeting any minute now.

GUM GIRL IN HAIR SCARE

All we need is a bit of proof the Evil Geniuses were behind the explosive bog roll incid—

Glurk!

What did you do that for? You almost—

Shhh.

28

You're a girl, Grace, how do they do that with their hair?

Never mind, I guess you wouldn't know.

Where is Cheryl? Those three are normally inseparable.

Hey, do you want to join the **Official Gum Girl Fan Club?**

GUM GIRL FAN CLUB

GUM GIRL FAN CLUB

Uh... that'd be weird.

Why? There's nothing weird about supporting Catastrophe's greatest superhero!

No, I'm sure she'd think it was really cool... Anyway, where's Cheryl?

I called her this morning, but there was no answer. Usually I get a text so we can co-ordinate outfits.

That's odd. Cheryl never ever misses school. Especially when there's a chance to show off.

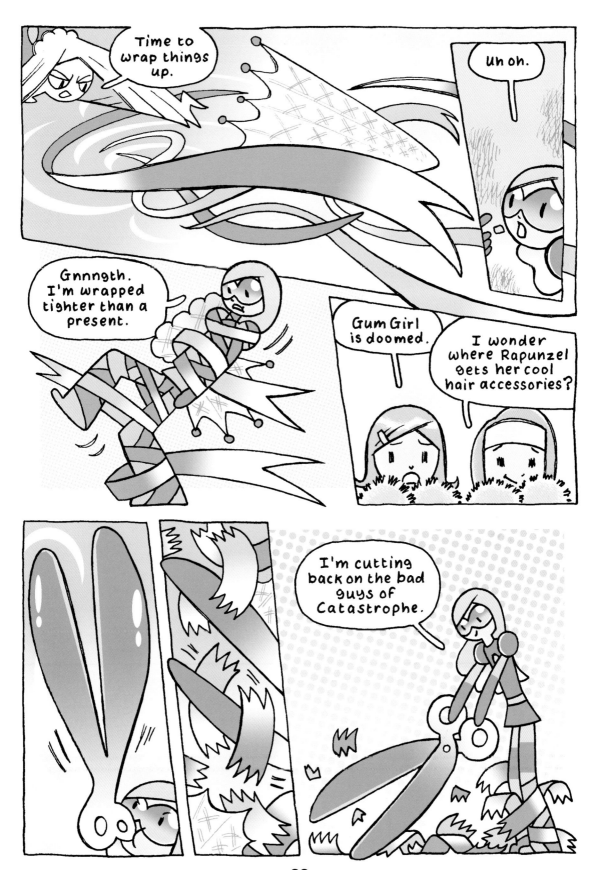

39

40

I do eat vegetables, I just don't like salad.

GUM GIRL in SALAD DAZE

Which vegetables do you like?

Um. Tomato soup?

Every single day you have a jam sandwich, apple and yoghurt in your lunch box. We want you to try some different foods.

You need your five-a-day or you won't grow up big and strong. I bet Gum Girl eats all her lettuce.

Wait until tomorrow, Grace, you'll learn to love your greens.

49

51

54

...CAESAR SALAD!

Panel 1:
TOP SECRET SALAD DRESSING

And I'll stop at nothing to make sure brats like you eat your veggies. If that means adding a little something extra to sweeten the pill, then so be it.

Panel 2:
Right. Well, I have to be off, I have maths in a minute.

58

59

63